Easter Island, Rapa Nui aged Facts and suppositions

Discovering the Points

Author

Sheun Parry

Copyright Notice

Table of Content

About Easter Island

Interesting Facts on Easter Island
Easter Island is one of the world's most famous yet least visited archaeological sites.

Easter Island is a small, hilly and treeless island of volcanic origin. It is located in the Pacific Ocean approximately 2200 miles (3600 kilometers) off the coast of the country of Chile, which owns the island.

Easter Island is sixty-three square miles in size and has three extinct volcanoes, the tallest rising to 1674 feet. Technically speaking, the island is a single massive volcano rising over ten thousand feet from the Pacific Ocean floor.

Easter Island History
The oldest known names of Easter island are Te Pito o Te Henua, meaning 'The Center of the World' and Mata-Ki-Te-Rani, meaning 'Eyes Looking at Heaven'.

In the 1860's Tahitian sailors gave the island the name Rapa Nui, meaning 'Great Rapa,' due to its resemblance to another island in Polynesia called Rapa Iti, meaning 'Little Rapa'.

The island received its current name, Easter Island, from the Dutch sea captain Jacob Roggeveen who was the first European to visit on Easter Sunday, April 5, 1722.

In the early 1950s, the Norwegian explorer Thor Heyerdahl (famous for his Kon-Tiki and Ra raft voyages across the oceans) popularized the idea that Easter Island had originally been settled by advanced societies of Indians from the coast of South America. Extensive archaeological, ethnographic and linguistic research has conclusively shown this hypothesis to be inaccurate.

It is now recognized that the original inhabitants of Easter Island were of Polynesian stock (DNA extracts from skeletons have confirmed this), that they most probably came from the Marquesas or Society islands, and that they arrived as early as 318 AD.

Easter Island Statues
Easter Island's most famous features are its enormous stone statues called moai, at least 288 of which once stood upon massive stone platforms called ahu. There are some 250 of these ahu platforms spaced approximately one half mile apart

to create an almost unbroken line around the perimeter of the island.

Another 600 moai statues, in various stages of completion, are scattered throughout the island. Nearly all the moai are carved from the hard stone of the Rano Raraku volcano.

The average moai statue is 14 feet, 6 inches tall and weighs 14 tons. Some moai were as large as 33 feet and weighed more than 80 tons. Depending upon the size of the statues, it is estimated that 50-150 people were needed to drag them across the countryside on sleds and rollers made from the island's trees.

A small number of the moai were once capped with 'crowns' or 'hats' of red volcanic stone. The meaning and purpose of these capstones is not known.

Easter Island Mysteries

Scholars are unable to explain the meaning and use of the moaistatues. It is assumed that their carving and erection derived from an idea rooted in similar practices found elsewhere in Polynesia but which evolved in a unique way on Easter Island. The statues may have been used for religious purposes.

Carved stone and wooden objects in ancient Polynesian religions, when properly fashioned and ritually prepared, were believed to have a magical spiritual essence called mana. Archaeologists have suggested that the moai statues of Easter Island were created with a similar purpose in mind.

Introduction

[The 'decline and fall' of Easter Island and its alleged self-destruction has become the poster child of a new environmentalist historiography, a school of thought that goes hand-in-hand with predictions of environmental disaster. Why did this exceptional civilisation crumble? What drove its population to extinction? These are some of the key questions Jared Diamond endeavours to answer in his new book 'Collapse: How Societies Choose to Fail or Survive.' According to Diamond, the people of Easter Island destroyed their forest, degraded the island's topsoil, wiped out their

plants and drove their animals to extinction. As a result of this self-inflicted environmental devastation, its complex society collapsed, descending into civil war, cannibalism and self-destruction. While his theory of ecocide has become almost paradigmatic in environmental circles, a dark and gory secret hangs over the premise of Easter Island's self-destruction: an actual genocide terminated Rapa Nui's indigenous populace and its culture. Diamond, however, ignores and fails to address the true reasons behind Rapa Nui's collapse. Why has he turned the victims of cultural and physical extermination into the perpetrators of their own demise? This paper is a first attempt to address this disquieting quandary. It describes the foundation of Diamond's environmental revisionism and explains why it does not hold up to scientific scrutiny].

Of all the vanished civilisations, no other has evoked as much bafflement, incredulity and conjecture as the Pacific island of Rapa Nui (Easter Island). This tiny patch of land was discovered by European explorers more than three hundred years ago amidst the vast space that is the South Pacific Ocean. Its civilisation attained a level of social complexity that gave rise to one of the most advanced cultures and technological feats of Neolithic societies anywhere in the world. Easter Island's stone-working skills and proficiency were far superior to any other Polynesian culture, as was its unique writing system. This most extraordinary society developed, flourished and persisted for perhaps more than one thousand years - before it collapsed and became all but extinct.

Why did this exceptional civilisation crumble? What drove its population to extinction? These are some of the key questions Jared Diamond endeavours to answer in his new book Collapse: How Societies Choose to Fail or Survive (Diamond, 2005) in a chapter which focuses on Easter Island.

Diamond's saga of the decline and fall of Easter Island is straightforward and can be summarised in a few words: Within a few centuries after the island was settled, the people of Easter Island destroyed their forest, degraded the island's topsoil, wiped out their plants and drove their animals to extinction. As a result of this self-inflicted environmental devastation, its complex society collapsed, descending into civil war, cannibalism and self-destruction. When Europeans discovered the island in the 18th century, they found a crashed society and a deprived population of survivors who subsisted among the ruins of a once vibrant civilisation.

Diamond's key line of reasoning is not difficult to grasp: Easter Island's cultural decline and collapse occurred before Europeans set foot on its shores. He spells out in no uncertain terms that the island's downfall was entirely self-inflicted: "It was the islanders themselves who had destroyed their own ancestor's work" (Diamond, 2005).

Lord May, the President of Britain's Royal Society, recently condensed Diamond's theory of environmental suicide in this way: "In a lecture at the Royal Society last week, Jared Diamond drew attention to populations, such as those on Easter Island, who denied they were having a catastrophic impact on the environment and were eventually wiped out, a phenomenon he called 'ecocide'" (May, 2005).

Diamond's theory has been around since the early 1980s. Since then, it has reached a mass audience due to a number of popular books and Diamond's own publications. As a result, the notion of ecological suicide has become the "orthodox model" of Easter Island's demise. "This story of self-induced eco-disaster and consequent selfdestruction of a Polynesian island society continues to provide the easy and uncomplicated shorthand for explaining the so-called cultural devolution of Rapa Nui society" (Rainbird, 2002).

The 'decline and fall' of Easter Island and its alleged self-destruction has become the poster child of the new environmentalist historiography, a school of thought that goes hand-in-hand with predictions of environmental disaster. Clive Ponting's The Green History of the World - for many years the main manifest of British eco-pessimism - begins his saga of ecological destruction and social degeneration with "The Lessons of Easter Island" (Ponting, 1992:1ff.). Others view Easter Island as a microcosm of planet Earth and consider the former's bleak fate as symptomatic for what awaits the whole of humanity. Thus, the story of Easter Island's environmental suicide has become the prime case for the gloomiest of grim eco-pessimism. After more than 30 years of palaeo-environmental research on Easter Island, one of its leading experts comes to an extremely gloomy conclusion: "It seems [...] that ecological sustainability may be an impossible dream. The revised Club of Rome predictions show that it is not very likely that we can put of the crunch by more than a few decades. Most of their models still show economic decline by AD 2100. Easter Island still seems to be a plausible model for Earth Island." (Flenley, 1998:127).

From a political and psychological point of view, this imagery of a complex civilisation self-destructing is overwhelming. It portrays an impression of utter failure that elicits shock and trepidation. It is in form of a shock-tactic when Diamond employs Rapa Nui's tragic end as a dire warning and a moral lesson for humanity today: "Easter [Island's] isolation makes it the clearest example of a society that destroyed itself by overexploiting its own resources. Those are the reasons why people see the collapse of Easter Island society as a metaphor, a worst-case scenario, for what may lie ahead of us in our own future" (Diamond, 2005).

While the theory of ecocide has become almost paradigmatic in environmental circles, a dark and gory secret hangs over the premise of Easter Island's selfdestruction: an actual genocide terminated Rapa Nui's indigenous populace and its culture. Diamond ignores, or neglects to address the true reasons behind Rapa Nui's collapse. Other researchers have no doubt that its people, their culture and its environment were destroyed to all intents and purposes by European slave-traders, whalers and colonists - and not by themselves! After all, the cruelty and systematic kidnapping by European slave-merchants, the near-extermination of the Island's indigenous population and the deliberate destruction of the island's environment has been regarded as "one of the most hideous atrocities committed by white men in the South Seas" (Métraux, 1957:38), "perhaps the most dreadful piece of genocide in Polynesian history" (Bellwood, 1978:363).

So why does Diamond maintain that Easter Island's celebrated culture, famous for its sophisticated architecture and giant stone statues, committed its own environmental suicide? How did the once well-known accounts about the "fatal impact" (Moorehead, 1966) of European disease, slavery and genocide - "the catastrophe that wiped out Easter Island's civilisation" (Métraux, ibid.) - turn into a contemporary parable of self-inflicted ecocide? In short, why have the victims of cultural and physical extermination been turned into the perpetrators of their own demise?

This paper is a first attempt to address this disquieting quandary. It describes the foundation of Diamond's environmental revisionism and explains why it does not hold up to scientific scrutiny.

Sheun Parry

Easter Island's Anonymity

Easter Island has probably been the subject of more hyperbole and speculation in proportion to its size than any other prehistoric place on Earth. Conjecture and bunkum might have been less significant but for the catastrophic end to the life of its people and the deliberate destruction of their culture which almost completely eradicated the memory of their own past.

Rapa Nui is the most isolated place of inhabited land in the world, located in the South Pacific. Separated by some 3,200 km from the nearest continent of South America, it was re-discovered in 1722 on Easter Day (hence its name) by the Dutch explorer

Jacob Roggeveen. At the time, the island was inhabited by a population of Polynesian origin who had arrived on Easter Island many centuries earlier. Due to the island's extreme remoteness (2,000 km separate it from the nearest inhabited island), the inhabitants depended on the island's endowment of natural and marine resources.

Diamond's historical reconstruction is based largely on fallacious mythologies and legends. He claims that Easter Island's civilisation had collapsed and the building From genocide to ecocide: the rape of Rapa Nui of its famous statues ceased long before 1722, and that a catastrophic civil war and population crash toppled its culture shortly before Europeans discovered Easter Island.

It is generally agreed that Rapa Nui's oral traditions are untrustworthy and of relatively late origin; they are extremely contradictory and historically unreliable. As Bellwood (1978) emphasises: "By the time detailed observations were made in the 1880s, the old culture was virtually dead [...] It is my own suspicion that none [of the traditions] are valid." Most of the information was "gleaned from a few surviving natives from the late nineteenth century onwards, by then decimated, demoralised and culturally impoverished population which had lost most of the collective cultural-historical memory" (Flenley and Bahn, 2003).

In spite of this widely-held consensus among researchers, Diamond insists that these highly questionable records are reliable. In his view, "those traditions contain much evidently reliable information about life on Easter in the century or so before European arrival" (Diamond, 2005:88). Without his confidence in the reliance on mythology and concocted folklore, Diamond would lack any evidence for pre-European civil wars, cannibalism and societal collapse. After all, there is no compelling archaeological evidence for any of the key claims of societal dissolution and breakdown before the 18th century (Rainbird, 2002). Only by relying on incongruous myths and contradictory tales can Diamond weave a superficially coherent reconstruction of Rapa Nui's prehistory.

To understand how Diamond arrived at the premise of Easter Island's environmental self-destruction, we need to examine the foundations of his theory and that of his precursors. Diamond is not the first to suggest that environmental degradation rather than European complicity destroyed Easter Island's civilisation. The scientific hypothesis of ecological breakdown goes back to the beginnings of the environmental movement and was originally developed in the 1970s and '80s. The historical roots of the problems that underline this idea, however, go back to the 18th century. Some of the island's most conspicuous "riddles" and "mysteries" were noticed by the first European visitors. How could 'naked savages' living on an ostensibly treeless island ever build, transport and erect giant stone sculptures? Who destroyed them and why? These and other questions have obsessed generations of adventurers.

The biggest problem faced by researchers who have attempted to answer these questions is the fact that the information written down by European discoverers and early visitors is extremely limited in content and reliability. Most of the early visitors only stayed for a few days. They never inspected the entire island, let alone study in detail the social infrastructure or the cultural and religious behaviour of its indigenous population. The accounts and reports that cover the period between Easter's discovery in 1722 and the extermination of its culture 150 years later are fundamentally inconsistent and contradictory. When, at the start of the 20th century, the first archaeological expeditions tried to reconstruct the island's history, they stumbled upon an exhausted terrain: the indigenous population had been almost completely annihilated, its culture and natural habitat destroyed as a result of physical, cultural and environmental obliteration.

Sheun Parry

Is Modernism Responsible of Civilization Downfall?

Easter Island's treeless landscape is perhaps the most crucial piece of physical evidence on which Diamond has based his theory of ecocide. Diamond's whole edifice of ecological self-destruction basically rests on Easter Island's deforestation. According to this premise, the extinction of the native palm tree triggered a series of environmental and social catastrophes that culminated in Easter Island's culture crash. As palms were cut down to clear land for agriculture, to plant gardens, to construct big canoes, to btain firewood for cooking and to transport and erect the giant cult statues, a cascade of environmental and societal knock-on disasters ensued.

Unquestionably, Rapa Nui has been devoid of large trees for quite some time. Pollen analysis has shown that palm trees once existed on the island and made up part of its flora. Despite this general agreement, research into both the causes and timing of deforestation remains contentious. Nunn (1999) has pointed out that there are numerous methodological problems involved in any attempt to reconstruct prehistoric human impact on the environment. Above all, natural events frequently generate changes that are sometimes similar if not identical to those produced by human impact. Numerous researchers (Finney, 1994; Hunter Anderson, 1998; Nunn, 1999; 2003; Orliac and Orliac, 1998) suggest that the climatic downturn caused by the Little Ice

Age may have exacerbated the problem of resource stress and could have contributed to the disappearance of the palm tree from Easter Island. There is little agreement on when exactly the island's palms became extinct.

Scientists disagree over which forces brought about deforestation and the degree of importance that palm trees may have played in Rapa Nui's culture compared to other tree species that survived into the early 20th century (Liller, 1995). The wrangle about the island's former tree cover goes back to the discovery of the island in 1722. When Jacob Roggeveen and his crew spotted Easter's imposing sculptures, he wondered how the natives could have created and erected them:

At first, these stone figures caused us to be filled with wonder, for we could not understand how it was possible that people who are destitute of heavy or thick timber, and also of stout cordage, out of which to construct gear, had been able to erect them; nevertheless some of these statues were a good 30 feet in height and broad in proportion. (Roggeveen, 1903:15).

The impression of a nearly treeless patch of land appears to be corroborated by Cornelis Bouman, Roggeveen's captain. In his log book, he stated that "of yams, bananas and small coconut palms we saw little and no other trees or crops" (von Saher, 1994:99). 'No thick timber, no strong ropes.' In other words, no means to transport and erect the giant statues. We see that Diamond's bewilderment goes back quite a while. Yet he often cites Roggeveen's and Bouman's impressions selectively. Most researchers deduce from their descriptions that Easter Island was totally deforested by 1722. But how could the discoverers have known that thick timber and strong ropes were wholly absent from the island? Their visit lasted just a few days and neither Roggeveen nor his crew inspected the whole of the island. And what about the small palm trees which Bouman claims to have seen - albeit few in numbers? What about the toromiro trees that existed on Easter Island until their modern extinction in the late 19th and early 20th centuries?

Diamond's assertion that Easter's discoverers encountered an island devoid of trees is also contradicted by Carl Friedrich Behrens, Roggeveen's officer. According to Behrens' description of the island and its inhabitants, the natives presented "palm branches as peace offerings." Their houses were "set up on wooden stakes, daubed over with luting and covered with palm leaves" (Behrens,

1903:134/135; his account was originally published in 1737).

Behrens concluded his remarkably cheerful description of Easter Island and its natural environment on a high note: "This island is a suitable and convenient place at which to obtain refreshment, as all the country is under cultivation and we saw in the distance whole tracts of woodland [ganze Wälder]" (Behrens, 1903:137).

Be that as it may, we should not place too much confidence in the contradictory accounts of early visitors who had only limited access and a few days to inspect the island, its people and its environment. Any selective reading of these accounts will inevitably result in an incoherent picture of the island's history.

Mulloy (1970) was one of the first to suggest that the fading and cessation of the megalithic culture could have been caused by deforestation. This suggestion was not out of the question. It was indirectly supported by pollen data analysed by the Norwegian expedition in the 1950s which showed that palm trees had once grown on the island (Heyerdahl and Ferdon, 1961).

In the 1980s, the first radio carbon analysis of peat and pollen samples attempted to establish tentatively at what time in history the process of deforestation transpired. Diamond and the researchers he cited face extreme uncertainty regarding one key question: when exactly did deforestation begin and, most importantly, when was it completed? Researchers who have analysed palm pollen suggest that the destruction of tree cover occurred "especially between 1200 and 800 BP, with the forest finally disappearing almost completely around 630 BP, say AD 1320" (Flenley, 1994:206; similar dates in Flenley, 1998; Flenley, 1984; King and Flenley, 1989).

"Therefore", Flenley (1998) argues, "the arrival of people could be causally related to the decline of trees, and the decline of trees could be causally related to the cultural collapse." However, confirming the existence of palm trees and palm fruits is one thing; linking their disappearance with an alleged societal collapse of the island's civilisation is an altogether different and much less convincing charge.

To begin with, Flenley's conspicuously early dating of Easter Island's deforestation created a major problem. Orliac and Orliac (1998) have called attention to this inconsistency: "If the trees had 'almost' completely disappeared by the 14th century, how could the statues be transported until the end of the 17th century?" In other words, if the destruction of palm trees triggered societal breakdown, why was the collapse of Easter Island's civilisation delayed by more than three centuries?

It was perhaps this palpable conundrum which forced Diamond to widen Flenley's early dates significantly. In a 1995 article, Diamond had claimed that "the fifteenth century marked the end not only for Easter's palm but for the forest itself [...] Not long after 1400 the palm finally became extinct, not only as a result of being chopped down but also because the now ubiquitous rats prevented its regeneration: of the dozens of preserved palm nuts discovered in caves on Easter, all had been chewed by rats and could no longer germinate." (Diamond, 1995).

This chronology, however, was not consistent with any causative link between deforestation and societal failure. For that reason, Diamond has moved the date of deforestation. While forest clearance "peaked around 1400", he has lengthened the island's forest cover by almost 200 years, which now reaches well into the 1600s. "After 1650 Easter's inhabitants were reduced to burning herbs, grasses and sugarcane scraps for fuel" (Diamond, 2005:108).

Writing in 1984, Flenley and his colleagues had emphasised that the alleged cessation of statue building "suddenly in AD 1680 [...] may have been caused by the extinction of the palm" (Dransfield, et al., 1984). Diamond adheres to this line of argumentation and links the loss of palm trees to the termination of the island's statue cult: "Lack of large timber and rope brought an end to the transport and erection of statues, and also the construction of seagoing canoes" (Diamond, 2005:107). What he fails to mention is that the disappearance of palms resulted neither in a lack of timber nor a lack of strong rope.

The disappearance of the palm, whenever it may have occurred, undoubtedly placed a considerable limit on Easter Island's ecology and culture, but what is highly questionable is Diamond's claim that the extinction of the palm tree automatically triggered societal collapse.

For a start, it remains unclear when exactly the last palm trees became extinct. Nobody questions that smaller trees existed on Easter Island up until the 20th century. There are even reports by European visitors, such as the testimony by J.L. Palmer (1870a) who claims to have spotted "boles of large palm trees" as late as the second half of the 19th century -

an observation confirmed by his co-visitor Lt Dundas who also saw "a few stumps of cocoa-nut palm" (Dundas, 1871). Given these and many other uncertainties, even Flenley himself wonders whether the palm may not have vanished until much later than generally thought: "Why did the palm become extinct? Possibly the coup de grace was administered by the sheep and goats introduced in the 19th and 20th centuries; but the species had clearly become rare before then, if Cook and La Pérouse are correct" (Flenley, 1993:35).

Needless to say, neither Cook nor La Pérouse are reliable witnesses given their extremely limited visits and incomplete knowledge of the island's natural setting. Whatever the case, deforestation was by no means an all-inclusive process. The smaller but important toromiro tree (Sophora toromiro) did not become extinct until the 20th century. It was essentially the only source of wood left to the islanders. Such trees provided the wood needed for housing, the building of small canoes, the carving of wooden figurines and other wooden tools and weapons. Many researchers are inclined to believe that wooden sledges or rollers produced from the toromiro tree also served as the apparatus for the statues' transportation. "The wood of the toromiro would have been suitable for rollers of 50 cm (20 in.) diameter, and also for levers, which were probably crucial to handling the statues" (Flenley and Bahn, 2003:123). Thus the disappearance of the palms, detrimental as it must have been, did not necessarily bring about an end to the building, transportation or erection of carved statues. Given that other timber was freely available as a replacement, there are no grounds to suggest that the disappearance of palms must have triggered civil war and societal collapse either.

Easter Island's Environment:

Prospective Delight or Wilderness?

It is difficult to reconstruct with any degree of confidence the ecology of Easter Island as it existed during the period between its discovery in 1722 and the start of the genocide that ultimately wiped out its civilisation. There are conflicting reports by early European visitors who landed on the island during the 18th century. The Dutch discoverers encountered a well-nourished, well-organized and populous people that resided among an environment which was well adapted to their needs.

Roggeveen maintained that Easter Island was exceptionally fertile. It produced large quantities of bananas, potatoes, and sugar-cane of extraordinary thickness. He concluded that, with careful cultivation, the island's productive soil and benign climate could be turned into an 'earthly paradise'. Captain Cook, on the other hand, was less impressed. When he visited the island 50 years later amidst high expectations (in all probability as a result of reading Behrens' upbeat report), he was disappointed by what he perceived to be an impoverished island. Yet, regardless of what may have happened in the aftermath of discovery and early visits, there are compelling reports from the late 18th century that Rapa Nui was far from being in a state of terminal decline. As Rollin, a major of the French expedition to Easter Island in 1786, underlined:

"Instead of meeting with men exhausted by famine, [...] I found, on the contrary, a considerable population, with more beauty and grace than I afterwards met in any other island; and a soil, which, with very little labour, furnished excellent provisions, and in an abundance more than sufficient for the consumption of the inhabitants" (Heyerdahl & Ferdon, 1961:57).

Yet Diamond does not provide a balanced account of these reports, depicting Easter Island's natural environment in the bleakest possible way: The island, when it was discovered, "was not a paradise but a wasteland"; it was devoid of timber, a windy place with few food sources and deficient "not just in coral-reef fish but in fish generally." Surely, he concludes, such an "impoverished landscape" could not have supported a complex and populous society capable of producing the impressive Neolithic architecture and giant statues.

This deliberately gloomy description is misleading in many respects. Neither is it an original slant but a rhetorical technique with a long history. The same one-sided arguments were raised for much of the 19th and 20th centuries. Writers who refused to accept that the native culture was capable of sophisticated skills and convoluted accomplishments had expressed the same doubts - as Métraux (1957) stressed almost half a century ago:

"Easter Island has often been pictured in the grimmest light. A barren island, a field of volcanic stones, an unproductive tract of land incapable of supporting a population of any density - such are the expressions most commonly used to describe it. By what strange freak did a brilliant civilization manage to develop on this supposedly barren rock? Is the transport of the greatest statues conceivable without trees required for the construction of skids or rollers? On what did the 'armies of slaves' live who hauled these statues over the fields of lava and along volcanic crests. [...] In reality, however, Easter Island's arid appearance is deceptive. Roggeveen considered it so fertile that he dubbed it an 'earthly Paradise'. M. de La Pérouse's gardener was delighted with the nature of the soil and declared that three day's work a year would be enough to support the population."

In sharp contrast to Diamond's gloomy description of the island's marine food supplies, Rapa Nui's coastal areas are rich in fish stocks. There are more than 100 species of which 95 per cent inhabit coastal areas. Also present are large numbers of lobsters which are much appreciated for their size and taste. The coasts are seasonally visited by marine reptiles such as the hawksbill turtle, the green turtle and the sea viper. Thomson, a U.S. Navy officer and Easter Island's first scientific researcher rightly emphasised the importance of abundant fish supplies for the native's prime diet:

"Fish has always been the principal means of support for the islanders, and the natives are exceedingly expert in the various methods of capturing them. The bonito, albicore, ray, dolphin, and porpoise are the off-shore fish most highly esteemed, but the swordfish and shark are also eaten. Rock-fish are caught in abundance and are remarkably sweet and good. Small fish of many varieties are caught along the shore, and the flying-fish are common. Eels of immense size are caught in the cavities and crevices of the rock-bound coast ... . Turtles are plentiful and are highly esteemed; at certain seasons a watch for them is constantly maintained on the sand beach. A species of crayfish is abundant. These are caught by the natives by diving into the pools among the rocks, and form an important article of food. Shell-fish are plentiful" (Thomson, 1891:458).

Fish hooks were made of stone and bone. Fishing nets were used, made from the paper mulberry tree. On numerous places around the coast, the natives had set up round towers built of stone that were said to be look-out towers from which watchers on land communicated the whereabouts of turtles and fish to those at sea. While fish was available in abundance, cultural practices restricted the periods during which fishing was allowed, thus preventing over-exploitation. Indeed, before the arrival of the deepsea fishing season "all fish living in twenty or thirty fathoms were considered poisonous" (Routledge, 1917:345).

Together with abundant and virtually unlimited sources of seafood, the cultivation of the island's fertile soil could easily sustain many thousands of inhabitants interminably. In view of the profusion of broadly unlimited food supplies (which also included abundant chickens, their eggs and the islands innumerable rats, a culinary 'delicacy' that were always available in abundance), Diamond's notion that the natives resorted to cannibalism as a result of catastrophic mass starvation is palpably absurd. In fact, there is no archaeological evidence whatsoever for either starvation or cannibalism.

The Reason for Renunciation of Original Civilization

"Could these primitive cannibals have been the masters who wrought the classical giant sculptures of aristocratic ruler type which dominated the countryside on this same island?", asked Thor Heyerdahl (1958:73) in one of his popular books on Easter Island. To be sure, one of the dominant themes and premises of past research on Easter Island's native population is the claim that the "primitive" inhabitants that were discovered in the 18th century could not have been the designers and architects of their civilisation's giant statues and architectural accomplishments.

Even broad-minded Westerners such as Captain Cook underestimated the technical prowess of the Polynesians in general. He could not believe, for example, that their seagoing canoes had overtaken him on fast passages (Lewis, 1972). When Cook visited Easter Island in 1774, he was equally suspicious about Rapa Nui's inhabitants: "We could hardly conceive how these islanders, wholly unacquainted with any mechanical power, could raise such stupendous figures, and afterwards place the large cylindric stones upon their heads" (Flenley and Bahn, 2003). Foster, who had accompanied Cook, also remarked that the statues "are so disproportionate to the strength of the nation, it is most reasonable to look upon them as the remains of better times".

For much of the last 300 years, Easter Island's indigenous population was considered to be 'savages' and 'degenerates', incapable of carving, transporting or raising the sculptures (moai) that symbolised the island's landscape. The inhabitants were declared uncivilised, uncultured or unable to have created their own, magnificent cultural icons. The giant statues could not have been assembled by a few 'savages': their construction would have required vast populations of epic proportion.

During the 19th and 20th century, many European writers attributed the features of this advanced culture to a superior, former race that became extinct, to sunken civilisations (such as the mythical continents of Atlantis or Mu) or to ancient societies in South America and the Middle East. The reconstruction of hypothetical cataclysms or imaginary migrations from ancient Peru, China or

India was based on a widely held perception and resulted in a sweeping conclusion: an outright denial that the indigenous population discovered on Rapa Nui were the real masterminds of their civilisation and its cultural features.

J.L. Palmer, who visited Easter Island in 1868, reported that the Jesuit missionaries who had established a mission four years earlier dissociated their flock of new converts from the 'pagan' culture of Rapa Nui. According to the missionaries, the giant statues "were the work of a former race" and that "the present one came here more recently, banished, it is said, from Oparo, or Kapa-iti, as they call it" (Palmer, 1868:372). Palmer was not entirely convinced by the Jesuits' assertion that the current inhabitants had nothing to do with the island's culture. The giant sculptures, he reasoned, were "apparently made by a race passed away, although it is possible that these people may have partially continued their construction and fabrication" (Palmer, 1870:110).

At the time, Palmer's presentation to the Royal Geographical Society divided his audience. One participant of the discussion that followed Palmer's talk "thought it was impossible to suppose that any people permanently established there would have been in the habit of constructing these giant works" and suggested that Peru was the origin of the island's civilisation (Palmer, 1870:116). Another participant countered "that the small wooden figures, which are still made and sold to visitors, bear a certain similarity to the stone images, which would scarcely exist if the present inhabitants were not immediately connected with the race that formed the earlier statues" (Palmer, 1870:118).

Sir George Grey finally demystified the whole debate by explaining the likely correlation between sufficient time and the large number of statues: "He thought it was extremely easy to account for the images of Easter Island, if the inhabitants had for centuries been Polynesians. If only eight or ten images were made in that number of years, a few centuries would suffice to cover the island with them" (Palmer, 1970:118). Perhaps the most celebrated promoter of the notion that Rapa Nui's culture was founded by a superior race - a white race that settled on the island prior to the Polynesian natives - was the Norwegian explorer Thor Heyerdahl. He developed his belief system long before he began to study Rapa Nui in situ. Heyerdahl was convinced that Easter Island had been settled by 'white-skinned' Caucasian people who had started off from Peru and Bolivia, but originated from a 'non-Semitic' race from the Middle East. Only after this first colonisation, a second wave of Polynesian settlers put down roots on the island (Heyerdahl, 1952).

Racially blinkered assumptions and misconceptions were the foundations of Heyerdahl's speculations about Easter Island: "The core of his Kon Tiki theory is that a white 'race' came from the Middle East to the Americas and then on to Polynesia to teach the dark-skinned people the arts of civilisation" (Holton, 2004).

Misleading Folklores and Invented Traditions

Easter Island has about 800 large statues, of which almost half remain unfinished in its main quarry. The question arose as to why so many statues were left unfinished, and when the last one was carved. The apparent cessation of statue production intimated that some devastating event or some great tragedy had brought an end to the island's customary life and traditional culture. What happened?

Diamond claims to possess the answer to this central question. According to his story line, the deforestation of Easter Island created dramatic societal consequences, culminating in mass starvation, a population crash, and a plunge into cannibalism. As the promises of the ruling elite and its statue cult could no longer be upheld, "the power of the chiefs and priests was overthrown around 1680 by military leaders called matatoa, and Easter's formerly complex integrated society collapsed in an epidemic of civil war" (Diamond, 2005:109). Not only the time-honoured ideology (which was "designed to impress the masses") failed; the old religion too was overthrown. It resulted in the abrupt and irrevocable termination of giant statue carving and culminated, around 1680, in an orchestrated campaign of rival clans who attacked and toppled one another's statues. More than anything else, it is this line of argument, this 'historical' piece of evidence, on which Diamond's entire edifice of Easter Island's 'ecocide' rests. However, he fails to acknowledge the dubious sources for this assertion.

When the first missionaries arrived on Rapa Nui in 1864, they found a dying culture in its final death throes. At the end of the century, hardly more than one hundred natives had survived the series of attacks, slave-raids, pandemics and destructions that had taken place for most of the 19th century. While Easter Island's populace was on the brink of extinction, its indigenous culture came to an end within less than four years. Exhausted from the ravages of genocide and unable to hold on to their vanishing traditions, the survivors surrendered to the calls of Christian missionaries. By 1868, the last survivors of a once stupendous civilisation had been converted.

The first fragmentary oral traditions were chronicled by European missionaries and visitors who interviewed a few locals about their 'pagan' history. It is important to understand the context of these early conversations. While the customary keepers of traditional folklore had been deported or killed, the island's ethnicity had changed as a result of population transfers on the 1860s and 70s, with an influx of a number of foreign Polynesians on Easter Island (Thomson, 1891:453). As Holton (2004) points out, "most of the island's myths were collected in the nineteenth century, after the population collapse." This was during a time when much of the cultural memory was "already contaminated by tales from Tahiti and the Marquesas, and elements of Christianity." Yet Diamond, who heavily relies on these unreliable records, fails to mention that these myths and legends were written down by Europeans after they had converted the survivors to their own belief system.

Notably, many of the new converts denied that the island's cultural icons - its imposing statues, its writing system - were the creation of their own society. According to Palmer's account of his conversation with the missionaries, the giant sculptures "were the work of a former race; the present one came here more recently" (Palmer, 1868). This curious and historically untenable form of cultural self-denial did not

receive much attention by the first historians of Easter Island. Nor was the crucial issue addressed of how the new belief system of these Christian converts may have shaped their attitude towards their 'pagan' past and its iconic 'idols'.

The few remains of Easter Island's traditional culture were finally brought to an end by activities of the missionaries and the traders who had arrived in their wake. "Missionization changed the culture to the point that within a year or two it no longer functioned in the traditional way. For purposes of indoctrination into Christianity, the 'pagan' natives were concentrated in a single settlement at Vaihu [...] thus effectively breaking the link to ancestral territories" (McCoy, 1976:147). The unique writing system that was discovered on wooden tablets on Easter Island during the 19th century did not survive the introduction of Christianity.

Easter's few survivors had no real historical recollection of most of the events that transpired prior to the annihilation of Rapa Nui's culture and its people in the 1860s and 70s. Routledge found that they had no idea whatever why the carving of statues had been abandoned. Instead they "invented a story which entirely satisfies the native mind and is repeated on every occasion" (Routledge, 1919:182). Most of Easter's legends and mythologies that were transmitted by European missionaries were originally inspired in the course of their campaign to convert the survivors of the 1860s deportations, slave labour and population crash. Given the evident fabrications found in a number of their accounts, it is extremely doubtful that any of the information is based on pre-historical events. In all likelihood, most stories are retrospective inventions that attempt to provide a mythical explanation of the present situation, in short, fabrications "which satisfies the native mind".

It is doubtful that the European missionaries and traders who settled on the island after the mass destruction (some of which went on even in the 1870s) felt any sense of guilt or shame in view of the appalling crimes. What is striking, nonetheless, is the conspicuous obsession of the missionaries and European visitors with Rapa Nui's pre- European history and antiquities. Two key questions dominated this new fixation: who were these ingenious builders of the vanished civilisation and who had exterminated them?

Given the racially prejudiced views of the time, it was perhaps not surprising that the search for an answer rummaged far into the past, focusing on ancient conflicts among 'savages' and tribal warfare - rather than exploring the most obvious and most recent reasons - that is to say the carnage and atrocities committed by European slavers, whalers and colonists.

It is generally agreed among judicious scholars that Easter Island's myths and legends transmitted and reported by European missionaries are unreliable. The same is true for the compilation of oral traditions collected under even shoddier conditions more than half a century later when Routledge and Métraux interviewed a few old natives. By that time, the inhabitants had absorbed the missionaries' teachings and doctrines. Not surprisingly, the first scientific expedition to Easter Island in 1914 found that hardly any reliable historical recollection remained among the few survivors. "The information given in reply to questions [about the history of the island] is generally wildly mythical, and any real knowledge crops up only indirectly" (Routledge, 1919:165).

Undoubtedly the most anomalous and dubious aspect of Easter's traditions is the apparent reticence about the island's most traumatic disaster in its entire history: the violent confrontations with European invaders and slave-raiders during much of the first half of the 19th century and the near-extinction of its people and their culture in the second half of this catastrophic century.

Katherine Routledge began to collect the island's traditions systematically during her expedition in 1914. She divided the legends into three groups: the first dealt with the legendary arrival of the islanders under their fabled culture-hero Hotu-matua; the second related to the extermination of the so-called Long-Ears a couple of generations after the legendary settlement; the third focused on the bloody wars, deportations and conflicts between two different groups of people, the Kotuu and Hotu Iti. According to the natives, the conflicts between various adversaries and invading enemies were squarely dated to the post-European period (Routledge, 1919: 277).

In his description of Easter Island's gory self-destruction, Diamond takes advantage of these legends of civil war, violence and societal collapse - but consigns them to the 17th century: "As their promises were being proved increasingly hollow, the power of the chiefs and priests was overthrown around 1680 by military leaders called matatoa, and Easter's formerly complexly integrated society collapsed in an epidemic of civil war" (Diamond, 2005:109).

It is extremely unlikely that the oral traditions of violence, deportation and genocide belong to the pre-European era, that is, two hundred years before the 19th century era when the natives experienced real attacks, violence, abductions and deportations. Diamond's theory of the island's self-destruction holds up only as long as the legendary traditions of violence and genocide are relocated to the time before the island's violent encounters with European visitors and raiders. That is why he disregards explicit testimony by the survivors of Rapa Nui's genocide. According to their accounts, they were "quite positive" that the ferocious events took place during the 19th century (Routledge, 1919:289) - and not, as Diamond asserts, 200 years earlier.

Where, then, does the story of civil war, bloody revolution and societal collapse in 1680 come from? As it happens, Diamond's theory is based on the fabrications of Thor Heyerdahl, an author who created and popularised an almost Orwellian-style pseudohistory of Easter Island's self-destruction - an event which he dated to 1680 no less.

Rapa Nui's Self-Destruction Saga

Thor Heyerdahl, Jared Diamond

Most authors who have written about Easter Island have acknowledged the enduring influence and popularity Heyerdahl's theories had during the second half of the 20th century. Diamond readily admits that his own interest in Easter Island "was kindled over 40 years ago by reading Heyerdahl's Kon-Tiki account and his romantic interpretation of Easter's history; I thought then that nothing could top that interpretation for excitement" (Diamond, 2005:82). Yet Heyerdahl's appeal was not just his eccentric romanticism; his narration contained a much darker, racialist streak. One cannot help but wonder how Diamond can be so blissfully oblivious of these connotations and the inadvertent influence they have asserted on his own depiction of Eastern Island's history.

To understand the similarities (and differences) between Heyerdahl's and Diamond's historical reconstructions, one must consider the views of those archaeologists and anthropologists who preceded Heyerdahl's paradigm of Rapa Nui's self-destruction. There is indeed a striking contrast between the position of those researchers who impugn European atrocities for the collapse of Rapa Nui's civilization and those (like Heyerdahl and Diamond) who blame the natives themselves for their demise. An examination of the viewpoints held by eminent researchers prior to Heyerdahl elucidates this point.

The Franco-Belgian expedition in 1934 led by Alfred Métraux and Henry Lavachery (Métraux, 1940) scrutinised Easter Island's statues in detail. The team tried to reconstruct the stylistic and historical evolution of statue building. Both researchers came to a reasonable - and some might say plausible - explanation of why the production of statues and the entire statue cult came to an end.

Lavachery divided the cultural history of statue production into five periods, the last of which corresponded with the disaster brought on by European slave-raids and the natives' subsequent near-extinction. He proposed that the carving of statues in the quarries actually continued until the sculptors and their customers were taken captive and hauled off from the island by whalers and slave-raiders in the 19th century (Lavachery, 1935). In short: "For a lack of orders, the sculptors did not finish the works they had begun, and as a result of the disaster that struck the island monumental sculpture disappeared" (Metraux, 1957:161).

This explanation was by far the most compelling reconstruction of the history and end of Rapa Nui's statues. Not only was there no solid evidence that the statue cult had come to an end by the time of European discovery in 1722 - in fact, the statue cult was still in practise during much of the 18th century. Unfortunately, the views by Métraux and Lavachery have been largely forgotten in contemporary discussions about the possible reasons for the cessation of the statue cult.

The main culprit for this amnesia was Heyerdahl and his imaginative rewriting of Easter Island's prehistory. His theory was a direct attack on the findings by Métraux and Lavachery. Not only had their research confirmed the Polynesian origins of Rapa Nui's indigenous culture; they also placed most of the blame for its destruction at the feet of Europeans. It was this two-fold conclusion that Heyerdahl attacked head-on after World War II - and which he finally succeeded to overturn.

Heyerdahl had organised an expedition in the mid 1950s and began excavations in order to prove his critics wrong. "Even before going to Easter Island he was determined to demonstrate the existence of a superior Caucasoid group as a substratum in Polynesia, and to his own satisfaction he naturally did so" (Bellwood, 1978:374). Corresponding to Routledge's three groups of myths and legends,

Heyerdahl's team divided Rapa Nui's "prehistory" into three racially distinct periods: an Early Period (AD 400-1100), a Middle Period (1100-1680) and a "decadent" Late Period (1680-1868).

It was Heyerdahl's conviction - based on his belief in the authenticity of these myths and oral traditions - that the large statues were produced by the superior Caucasian settlers during what he called the Middle Period. These were members of a race of "light-skinned" people who were called 'Long-Ears' due to their large plugs that elongated their earlobes. According to Heyerdahl's race theory, they constructed the stone statues, cutting them in their own image (Holton, 2004). It was during this imaginary zenith of the island's civilisation that the "dark-skinned" Polynesian migrants arrived. After centuries of peaceful coexistence, conflicts between the two races mounted and finally culminated in a war of extermination. Relying on dubious and largely unreliable genealogies put together by the island's parish priest, Father Sebastian Englert (1948/1970), Heyerdahl maintained that the legendary "race war" resulted in the extermination of the light-skinned 'Long-Ears' by their dark-skinned adversaries and the termination of the statue cult in AD 1680 (Heyerdahl and Ferdon, 1961). Thus, the mythological civil war which caused the collapse of the statue cult plays a decisive role in Heyerdahl's racial history of Easter Island's collapse. It is important to understand the implications of Heyerdahl's revisionism.

According to his plot, the destruction of Rapa Nui's statue cult and its complex society was not the fault of European perpetrators. On the contrary, he blamed the natives for their own demise: Heyerdahl claimed that shortly before the arrival of the Europeans, in 1680 to be precise, a civil war had already led to Easter Island's self-destruction. During the last few decades, genetic, linguistic and archaeological research has essentially ruled out his claim of two separate settlement movements by two distinct populations. Yet in spite of overwhelming rejection of his theories, Heyerdahl's key premise - that of a civil war around 1680 - is generally accepted by Diamond and most of his contemporaries. Even some of his foremost critics who blame climatic changes during the Little Ice Age rather than human action for Easter Island's deforestation consent to Heyerdahl's story line of civil war and societal collapse in the 17th century (Orliac and Orliac, 1998:132).

Diamond also seems prepared to accept Heyerdahl's erroneous dating of these mythological events. Oral traditions allege that a major battle between the Long-Ears and the Short-Ears took place shortly after the island's original settlement at the so-called Poike Ditch, a series of trenches of natural or human origin. Heyerdahl's expedition in 1955 discovered what appeared to be a 'burned' zone. Charcoal remains found in this location were radiocarbon-dated and yielded a date of AD 1676 +/- 100. It was decided that this piece of evidence was confirmation of the reality of the "war of extermination" and that it must have happened in 1680. Hence, Edwin Ferdon, a member of Heyerdahls' expedition, concluded: "The AD 1680 date, dividing the Middle from the Late Period, is based upon the C-14 date obtained from the large charcoal deposit in the Poike Ditch. This carbon is believed to be the remains of the great fire made during the battle that legend says took place here" (Ferdon, 1961:527).

While oral tradition had located this mythical event at the very beginning of the island's history,

Heyerdahl now moved it to its very end, just before its rediscovery by Roggeveen. Easter Island's history was rewritten accordingly. For Heyerdahl, AD 1680 was a scientifically significant date, providing unambiguous evidence which seemed to confirm what he had believed all along: "The Late Period, a decadent phase, begins with the great Poike ditch fire and the abrupt cessation of statuary carving at Rana Raraku" (Heyerdahl, 1961:497). But was the charcoal really proof of warfare? Wasn't it just a piece of burned wood, perhaps entirely unconnected to any historical event? The clue to Diamond's reconstruction of civil war and societal collapse is found here: it is based on Heyerdahl's creative dating and its speculative correlation.

Subsequent research revealed that neither the "burned zone" nor the tentative dates could be confirmed. "More recent excavations in the ditch uncovered only root and vegetable moulds and a tree hole with charcoal [...] which gave a radiocarbon date in the eleventh century AD, which seems to cast the gravest doubt on this 'ditch' having been involved in a battle of the type and date mentioned in the traditions" (Flenley and Bahn, 2003:153/54).

In other words, the very foundation of Heyerdahl's civil war and societal breakdown in 1680 has been comprehensively debunked. Notwithstanding this rejection, the modern myth of a 17th century civil war between indigenous tribes and societal collapse before the arrival of the first Europeans remains an almost universally accepted core belief among Easter Island historians and researchers.

But there are more reasons to doubt Diamond's claims. His reconstruction of events also contradicts more reliable historical accounts. Métraux (1957) recorded many oral histories of tribal warfare. These accounts demonstrate that the fighting which engulfed the island occurred in the aftermath of European contact. After all, Easter Island's statues were still standing in 1722. What is not entirely clear, however, is whether these vague and predominantly fickle accounts refer to inter-tribal conflicts among the indigenous population, or whether they also include reflections of the historically documented battles with European whalers and slave-traders.

Be that as it may, in view of the evidence that confirms a post-European date for the end of the statue cult, some new light should be shed on the traditions regarding the 'legendary' extermination of the Long-Ears. After all, this saga was fundamentally an attempt to explain the disappearance of a large section of Rapa Nui's indigenous population. Evidently, there was a recollection that they were wiped out by their enemies. The question is: could this tradition reflect real events that actually happened to the historical 'Long-Ears' in the not so distant past? Métraux (1957:228) seems to hint at a genocidal explanation when he contrasts the legendary date of the stories with real, historical events:

"The historical conclusions drawn from this tale are disconcerting when we recall that the 'Long-Ears', so brutally exterminated by their rivals in the seventeenth century, were seen and described by voyagers in the eighteenth and nineteenth centuries. For at this time all the Easter Islanders had long ears, if by this is meant that they deformed the lobe of the ear so as to insert heavy ornaments."

According to Métraux, the last 'long-eared' Easter Islander perished in the nineteenth century -

together with the last remnants of a once brilliant civilisation. Evidently, the Long-Ears were not exterminated as a result of a mythical civil war but due to the atrocities committed by Europeans.

Diamond also employs archaeological evidence for his claim of the pre-European date of civil war and societal collapse. He refers to obsidian points (mataa) as indicators of increased fighting as a result of environmental degradation. Their exact dating, however, remains ambiguous. Bahn and Flenley (1992:165) point out that these spear points only "proliferated in the 18th and 19th centuries when they became the commonest artefact on the island".

The implications of archaeological evidence thus contradict Diamond's argument that the collapse occurred prior to Easter's traumatic collision with European visitors and attackers. Rainbird (2002:446) emphasises: "It thus appears from the evidence presented by Bahn and Flenley themselves that the majority of the major indicators of apparent competition, warfare, and social disarray, apparently caused by islander-induced ecodisaster, dates to the decades and centuries following initial European visits."

Diamond's speculations regarding population pressure and the lack of an escape valve appear equally implausible. As long as canoes were available, emigration from the island was not only possible; it must have been a near certainty imposed by victorious tribes or a chance for young men to demonstrate their courage. After all, maritime expansion had occurred throughout Polynesia. In short, population pressure would not necessarily lead to civil war.

Nor is there any solid evidence for any population pressure or pre-19th century population crash. In fact, some of the most fertile areas with the best water supply (in close proximity to the large fresh-water late of the Rano Kau crater) were never used or indeed needed for agriculture (McCoy, 1976:154); they never saw any permanent habitation, a fact that is at odds with Diamond's claim of overpopulation, soil erosion or diminished crop yields.

Easter Island presents a problem because the case for demographic decline caused by anthropogenic environmental devastation is insufficiently documented at critical points. All estimates of the peak size of the prehistoric population are entirely speculative; it may never have exceeded the 2000-3000 that can be estimated from early historical records. Warfare was endemic on most Polynesian islands and does not indicate demographic collapse. (Anderson, 2002:382)

So, is there any compelling evidence for Diamond's belief in extensive and prevalent warfare before the onset of the European disaster? In contrast to Diamond's claims, osteological data (i.e. bone pathology and osteometric data from human skeletons) found on Easter Island show no palpable evidence of widespread or chronic civil war:

"The impression given by folklore and sporadic historical documentation is of chronic, lethal warfare during the late prehistoric and early historic periods. Based on the osteological evidence, this assessment is somewhat misleading. Fractures indicative of cranial trauma are fairly common, and examples of fatal injuries are evident; however, most skeletal injuries appear to have been nonlethal. Few fatalities were directly attributable to violence. The physical evidence suggests that the frequency of warfare and lethal events was exaggerated in folklore, presumably because of its horrific results and importance in the daily lives of participants." (Owsley et al., 1994:)

In brief, there is little if any archaeological evidence for pre-European civil war or societal collapse. On the other hand, there is forceful evidence to suggest that the natives' recollections of warfare and violent conflict most likely belong to the hostilities in the wake of European attacks on the island. They may conceivably be linked to tribal conflicts that resulted from societal breakdown and the apparent transfer of foreign populations which occurred in the 1860s. Whatever the case may be, Heyerdahl's erroneous dating of a mythological civil war to the year 1680 forms a cornerstone of Diamond's narrative of Easter

Island's self-destruction, without which there is no solid evidence for either civil war or societal collapse.

"A carnage of Internecine Warfare and Anthropophagy"?

Given Diamond's self-declared ecological commitment, it is not surprising to find that his views on what he has called Easter Island's self-inflicted "holocaust" were fully formed long before he started to study the island's history in any great detail. The blueprint for "Collapse" and its key thesis of 'ecological suicide' goes back to his first bestseller, published in 1991 under the Gibbon-esque title "The Rise and Fall of the Third Chimpanzee" (Diamond, 1991). On one page, and without much elaboration,

Diamond asserted that Easter Island's "society collapsed in a holocaust of internecine warfare and cannibalism" as a result of deforestation and soil erosion.

In Collapse, Diamond attempts to buttress this core premise with reference to selective data and arguments. Failing to assess many of the contentious issues in an even-handed and impartial manner, he approaches scientific problems from the standpoint of an environmental campaigner and inevitably arrives at flawed conclusions.

This deficiency in scrutiny and critical analysis is particularly apparent in his treatment of alleged cannibalism among Easter Island's indigenous population. Already in 1995, he contended that civil war and starvation drove the natives to eat each other:

"They also turned to the largest remaining meat source available: humans, whose bones became common in late Easter Island garbage heaps. Oral traditions of the islanders are rife with cannibalism; the most inflammatory taunt that could be snarled at an enemy was "The flesh of your mother sticks between my teeth." (Diamond, 1995)

Throughout his writings, Diamond seems obsessed with what Arens (1979) calls the Man-Eating Myth, a gullible belief unsupported by any empirical evidence. Just as his certainty in the folklore of pre-European civil war and collapse is based on his confidence in myth and legend, Diamond's fascination with the island's "holocaust of cannibalism" relates to his acceptance of unreliable sources.

A closer examination of his claims reveals that the accusation of "cannibalism" was a European fabrication invented during a time when European whalers and raiders repeatedly attacked the island's population. The allegation first surfaced in 1845 in a report in the French journal L'univers. According to the sensationalist tabloid-style story, the young commander of a French vessel that had landed on Easter Island fortuitously "escaped being the victim of cannibals.... Mr Olliver was brought back on board; his whole body was covered with wounds. He had, on various parts of his body, the teeth marks of these cruel islanders, who had begun to eat him alive" (Fischer, 1992: 73).

Most researchers concur that this horror-story is most likely a hoax, "one of the most ridiculous yarns ever spun about the island" (Bahn, 1997), in short the fictional fantasy of mid-nineteen century European bigotry. Nevertheless, the anecdote appears to have had a significant impact on the French missionaries who were the first Europeans to settle on the island about 20 years after the reported incident. It is from their reports and allegations that we hear about the practice of cannibalism among the natives. More importantly, the French missionaries invoke the traditional claim that cannibalism was rampant among Easter's population until the introduction of Christianity (Métraux, 1940:150).

The mere fact that some converts to Christianity later accused their pagan ancestors of engaging in cannibalism can hardly be taken as adequate evidence for the practices. After all, the converts had absorbed the new creed and its teachings which inevitably tainted their views of the 'detestable' past of their pagan culture. What is more, admitting to cannibalism may have played an important part of the 'dialogue' with their European masters, perhaps as a "weapon of terror, one of the few weapons they possessed in an unequal contest" (Hulme, 1998: 23).

Bahn (1997), who has critically evaluated the missionaries' dubious reports of alleged cannibalism, points out that "it is certainly noteworthy that none of the early European visitors before the missionaries ever alluded to the practice." Most importantly, the first scientific exploration of the island in 1914 confirmed that the indigenous population vehemently denied that they (or their 'fathers') had ever been cannibals (Routledge, 1919).

Despite the lack of any empirical evidence and notwithstanding prevalent scepticism, Diamond bolsters his allegation of cannibalism because it reinforces his horror-scenario of an ecological 'holocaust'. Contemporary ethnographical research, however, has confirmed that there is hardly any tangible evidence for the existence of cannibalism (other than individual) "anywhere, in any period" (Flenley and Bahn, 2003:157). Given the extreme rarity of cannibalism 'anywhere, in any period', the so-called 'oral traditions' shaped by European missionaries and their converts about its practice on Easter Island should be discarded once and for all.

Sheun Parry

The Failure: Easter Island's Disremembered Massacre

The slave raids during the 1860s and the enforced population transfers of the 1870s had a crushing impact on Easter Island. They decimated the island's population and shattered its culture. Despite hundreds of books and thousands of papers on the 'mysteries' of Easter Island, this genocide which wiped out Rapa Nui's civilisation has been largely ignored. As a matter of fact, nobody to date has written a detailed history of these traumatic events.

The striking lack of research into actual European atrocities contrasts noticeably with the fixation of most researchers on hypothesised ecological 'suicide' which is squarely blamed on the self-destructive actions of the natives themselves. As a result, our knowledge about the exact number, gravity and detrimental consequences of the more than 50 European incursions on Easter Island during the 19th century remains extremely incomplete. We don't even know whether the island's population - before it crashed in the 1860s and 70s - stood at 3,000, 5,000 or as high as 20,000, a dubiously high estimate provided by A.A. Salmon who was the first to take a population census in 1886 (Thomson, 1891:460).

What is undisputed, however, is that as a result of the series of slave raids, the subsequent small pox pandemics and numerous population transfers of the 1860s and '70s, the population was chopped down to a mere 100-odd survivors in 1877. Between the first European contact in 1722 and the beginning of the Peruvian slave raids in 1862, some 53 European vessels called at Easter Island (McCall, 1976). Most probably, other ships visited the island without our knowledge. What attracted these ships? "The greatest resources of the island were the people themselves, whom the Europeans viewed as sources of labor and, in the case of women, sexual satisfaction" (Owsley, 1994:163). Sporadically, whaling ships also abducted islanders to replace or supplement crew members. Given what we know about the often violent assaults of early visitors, whalers and the raids of slave traders on the native population, it is likely

that many atrocities went unrecorded. From what little we do know, an appalling picture of indisputable genocide and ecocide emerges. Murder, rape, mass deportation and repeated attempts to destroy the island's environment characterised the poignant history of Rapa Nui during much of the 19th century (Owsley, 1994; Maziere, 1969).

The year 1805 saw the first in a series of slave-raids when the captain of the New- London Schooner Nancy landed on Easter Island with the intention of kidnapping labour slaves. After a bloody battle with the natives, the crew managed to abduct 12 native men and 10 women (the exact numbers of those killed and deported are unknown). Between 1815 and 1825, three further traumatic encounters with intruders and slave-raiders resulted in battles and warfare-like conflicts between Europeans and natives. According to some ship logs and accounts of sailors, Rapa Nuians drove back European visitors on a number of occasions by attacking and repelling them. Given these recurring and war-like skirmishes (which also included the premeditated kidnapping and rape of women), it is probable that some of the oral tradition of tribal conflict and warfare may reflect also these traumatic clashes, many of which led to heavy casualties among the native defenders. By the 1830s, whalers reported that sexually-transmitted diseases had become a chronic peril on Easter Island (Routledge, 1919).

In October 1862, two marauding ships landed on Easter Island in search for slave labourers. The crew seized and captured 150 natives and transferred them to Peru where they were sold as slaves for an average price of $300 (Englert, 1948/1970). Between December 1862 and March 1863, an estimated 1,000-1,400 native people (the actual number is unknown) were captured and deported by Peruvian and Spanish slave-raiders (Thomson, 1891:460; Owsley et al., 1994). Among them were King Kamakoi and his son. It is believed (but by no means certain) that almost 90% died in the following weeks and months of diseases and maltreatment. Due to international protests, Peru repatriated around one hundred Polynesians who had survived the horrors of slave labour, although some of those selected for repatriation probably originated from other Polynesian islands (a policy that was not unusual at the time in order to instigate tribal conflicts and confusion). According to some later accounts, 100 or so slave labourers were shipped back to Easter Island, but most of them died on their way from smallpox.

"Only fifteen regained the island, to the greatest misfortune of the population that had been left behind; shortly after their return, smallpox, the germs of which they had brought with them, broke out and transformed the island into a vast charnelhouse. Since there were too many corpses to bury in the family mausoleums, they were thrown down clefts in the rock or dragged into underground tunnels. [...] Civil war added their toll to the havoc wrought by this murderous epidemic. The social order had been undermined, the fields were left without owners, and people fought for possession of them. Then there was famine. The population fell to about six hundred. The majority of members of the priestly class disappeared, taking with them the secrets of the past. The following year, when the first missionaries settled on the island, they found a culture in its death throes: the religious and social system had been destroyed and a leaden apathy weighed down the survivors from these disasters." (Métraux, 1957, 47)

With the deportation and deaths of the hereditary tribal and community leaders, the social and religious system disintegrated. The old social order of Easter

Island had been entirely destroyed. Internal strife and tribal fighting that occurred when relatives of deported and dead islanders clashed over their property and land rights in 1863 and 1864 finally led to societal collapse and starvation. Much of Rapa Nui's traditions of internal violence and warfare that were collected, infered and construed many decades and generations later by European researchers are most plausibly collective reflections and individual recollections of these extremely traumatic clashes - and not accounts of some mythical events many hundreds of years earlier.

As if this cataclysmic population crash and the collapse of Rapa Nui's society wasn't enough, renewed slave-raids on the survivors commenced in the 1870s. These attacks resulted in brutal conflict with shootings and casualties and culminated in a genuine ecocide. In a deliberate attempt to empty

Rapa Nui of its last remnants of indigenous population, two European traders, J.B. Dutroux-Bornier and J. Brander, agreed to remove the entire remaining population to Tahiti. Their houses were burnt and destroyed. "After burning the natives' huts, Dutroux-Bornier had all their sweet potatoes pulled out of the ground three times, to facilitate the persuasion of the starving natives who had thus little hope of surviving on their own island" (Heyerdahl and Ferdon, 1961:76).

By 1877, the annihilation of Rapa Nui's civilisation was practically complete: most of those who had survived the atrocities, pandemics and ecocide were transported to Tahiti, leaving behind just one-hundred odd natives. Ten years later, after Chile officially annexed the island in 1888, the few survivors of Rapa Nui's forgotten genocide were forced into a detention centre in the village of

Hangaro, a camp where they were kept confined under the most appalling conditions for nearly 100 years:

"It was surrounded by a barbed-wire enclosure with two gates in it, and no one was allowed to pass through them without the permission of the Chilean military leader. At six in the afternoon these gates were locked...These regulations have remained almost unchanged...In 1964, 1,000 surviving Easter islanders [were] living in the most unbelievable wretchedness and lack of freedom." (Maziere, 1969: 35)

The physical destruction of one of mankind's most illustrious civilisations and its people occurred during much of the 19th and 20th centuries. These atrocities took place in the open. They were witnessed, recorded and decried by many observers. Yet the disappearance of Rapa Nui's civilisation has generated a myriad of bizarre theories and wild speculations, most of which focus on what is often regarded as its "mysterious" culture and its "puzzling" downfall. The real mystery of Easter Island, however, is not its collapse. It is why distinguished scientists feel compelled to concoct a story of ecological suicide when the actual perpetrators of the civilisation's deliberate destruction are well known and were identified long ago.

In Conclusion

Throughout his writings, Diamond maintains that he is reasonably hopeful about the future of humanity. Nevertheless, he does not hesitate to foretell environmental calamity and societal breakdown in the most unhinged imagery: "By the time my young sons reach retirement age, half the world's species will be extinct, the air radioactive, and the seas polluted with oil ... I have no doubt that any humans still alive in the radioactive soup of the Twenty-second Century will write equally nostalgically about our own era" (Diamond, 1991:285).

It is this profound anxiety about the future and its impact on the environment that stirs Diamond's writings and imagination. Regrettably, his eagerness to forestall doom often clouds his ability to assess historical and archaeological evidence in an impartial, even-handed approach. This fixation bears a striking resemblance to other authors who have tried to apply other standardised theoretical models to Easter Island history.

In a powerful critique of the methods applied by Heyerdahl and a number of other authors, Bahn has highlighted a fundamental problem of contemporary research on Easter Island: "The authors make their assumptions. They then look for evidence, pick out the bits they like, ignore the bits that don't fit, and finally proclaim that their assumptions have been vindicated" (Bahn, 1990:24). A similar criticism can be made of Diamond's eco-biased approach to the question of Rapa Nui's collapse.

In many ways, Diamond's methodological approach suffers from a manifest lack of scientific scrutiny. Instead of carefully weighing up and critically assessing the quality, authenticity and reliability of the data he employs to support his arguments, he consistently selects only the data and interpretations that seem to confirm his conviction that Easter Island self-destructed. Within science, this method is generally

known as Confirmation Bias, an often inadvertent mental process among researchers "which refers to a type of selective thinking whereby one tends to notice and to look for what confirms one's beliefs, and to ignore, not look for, or undervalue the relevance of what contradicts one's beliefs" (Carroll, 2003).

There can be little doubt that on a number of occasions indigenous populations have destroyed animal species and seriously degraded parts of their habitats. Thus, my criticism of Diamond's eco-pessimism does not rest on an unjustifiable belief in what he calls the "Rousseau-esque fantasy" of the 'ecological noble Savage' (Ellingson, 2001). The fundamental flaw in his treatment of Easter Island is that he approaches the problems of its evolution and history with the zeal of an environmental campaigner, and not with the dispassionate detachment of a scientist. He is too much inclined to employ his historical reconstructions as a tool for the environmental agenda and subordinates much of his analysis to moralistic and preconceived intentions.

According to Diamond (1991), the attack on what he calls the "progressive party line" seeks to "demolish another sacred belief: that human history over the last million years has been a long tale of progress". Instead of the old mantra of preordained advancement and perfection, the progressive dogmatism he admits he grew up with, Diamond claims to have uncovered a new principle: that human history has been beset with self-inflicted environmental disasters, ecological degradation and cultural degeneration. For an author who famously claimed to have turned history into a science, it is quite remarkable to see a complete lack of awareness about the fact that his brand of 'eco-pessimism' has deep historical roots (Herman, 1997).

Collapse is perhaps the prime upshot of the amalgamation of environmental determinism and cultural pessimism in the social sciences. It epitomises a new and burgeoning doctrine expounded largely by disillusioned left-wingers and former Marxist intellectuals. In place of the old creed of class warfare and socio-economic driving forces that used to explain every single development under the sun, environmental determinism essentially applies the same one-sided rigidity to historical events and societal evolution (Peiser, 2003).

As a final point, I would argue that Easter Island is a poor example for a morality tale about environmental degradation. Easter Island's tragic experience is not a metaphor for the entire Earth. The extreme isolation of Rapa Nui is an exception even among islands, and does not constitute the ordinary problems of the human environment interface. Yet in spite of exceptionally challenging conditions, the indigenous population chose to survive - and they did. They tackled the problems of a difficult and challenging environment which both geography and their own actions forced upon them. They successfully adapted to changing circumstances and did not show any signs of terminal decline when they were discovered by Europeans in 1722.

There is no reason to believe that its civilization could not have adapted and survived (in a modified form) to an environment devoid of large timber. What they could not endure, however, and what most of them did not survive, was something altogether different: the systematic destruction of their society, their people and their culture. Diamond has chosen to close his eyes to the real culprits of Rapa Nui's real collapse and annihilation. As Rainbird (2003) aptly concludes: "Whatever may have happened in the past on Easter Island, whatever they did to their island themselves, it totally pales into insignificance compared to the impact that was going to come through Western contact.